FBA

PRODUCT SOURCING

BLUEPRINT

How to Find, Evaluate, and Hire the Best Suppliers
at the Best Prices for Your Fulfillment by Amazon Business

Red Mikhail

TABLE OF CONTENTS

Introduction

Welcome to Part 4 of the Amazon FBA Business Series – FBA Product Sourcing Blueprint. In part 1, we talked about the AMAZON FBA business in general and how a beginner can get started even without huge capital or experience. In part 2, we discussed the importance of product research and how you can find products that has a higher chance of being profitable. And in part 3, we discussed the role of keyword research on your FBA business and I taught you the best strategies for doing keyword research without using any paid tools.

In this book, we are going to focus our attention on finding suppliers, negotiating the best prices, shipping our products and making sure that it reaches Amazon's fulfillment center so we can start selling it on Amazon.com as soon as possible.

In case you haven't got the chance to read part 1 to part 3 yet, I would highly recommend that you start with them as they would serve as great foundational knowledge for the lessons to come. They are all available in eBook, paperback and audiobook format.

So, who is this book for?

It is for people who already have a basic idea of how ecommerce works and someone who already have a product in mind. We won't discuss product research in this book so you might want to get a handle of that part first if you don't have any idea what product to sell yet. However, if you already have something in mind, then this book will be crucial to your FBA journey.

Finding product suppliers is where most people get stuck. It's understandable because this is where you put your money where your mouth is. This is the part where you invest in product samples and your first order.

Depending on the product you chose, that would likely cost between $500-$5,000.

So yeah, your business isn't just an idea anymore – your physical product now makes it real.

Now, I don't want you to be afraid of the process because it can be pretty simple as long as you follow the guidelines and steps that I'm going to discuss in this book.

Here's an overview of the whole process.

Chapter 1 - Researching Suppliers

First, I'll show you how to research the best suppliers and I'll give you 5 of the best ways to find quality suppliers that won't take advantage of you.

What criteria do you have to follow so you can pick the best suppliers for your product? I will reveal all of that in this chapter.

Chapter 2 – Hiring the Best Suppliers

Next, I'll teach you how to veto your suppliers so you know that you're only dealing with legit ones. You won't want to get scammed for $5,000 for your first order, don't you? In this chapter, I'll show you how to make the initial contact and what questions to ask to know if they are a legit manufacturer or not.

Chapter 3 – Ordering Units, Negotiating for the Best Prices and the Shipping Process Explained

In this chapter, I'll give you the steps that you need to take to make sure that you are making the right order for your product. I will also give you a checklist of things to remember before you finalize your order. This will also help you avoid losing money which most first-time sellers do.

In this chapter, I'll also teach you how to negotiate for the best prices where you'll both come out feeling like a winner.

In addition, we'll also discuss the all-too confusing shipping process where most people get into a lot of trouble for.

What's the process of shipping from your supplier to your address or Amazon's fulfillment center? What you do actually do each time you have a shipment ready to sell on AMAZON FBA? Follow my lead and I guarantee that you'll have a much seamless process of getting your products to Amazon's fulfillment center.

Chapter 4 – Barcodes and FBA Fees Demystified

In chapter 4, we'll talk about how to set up your Barcodes, how they work, and how to calculate your FBA fees.

And lastly, in **Chapter 5**, we'll discuss the best **Practices of the Most Profitable Ecommerce Business Owners** as it relates to finding the best suppliers, dealing with suppliers and making the shipping process as seamless as possible.

Think of these are your personal guidelines to follow so you won't lose your shirt in this business.

The Importance of Finding Great Suppliers

Finding great suppliers isn't exactly rocket science. It takes a bit of practice to master and you'll still probably make some mistakes even if you follow every single thing I say in this book. And that's perfectly fine. In fact, you should expect this process to be hard. If it's easy, then everybody would do it and this business wouldn't be as profitable as it is. The good news is finding great suppliers is a learnable skill. If you're willing to make an investment in time, money and effort – then I don't see any reason why you won't succeed. With the right product and the right supplier, you can build a business that would still exist 3,5 10 or even 20 years from now. A business that will feed your family, pay for your vacations, and buy your heart's desire. But then again, it's not as easy as ABC. If you're willing to go through learning pains, then I have a feeling that you will be one of the people who will still be thriving in this business years from now.

I hope I didn't scare you into quitting! Ha ha.
If I did, then this business is probably not for you.

If you're still here, then allow me to show you the way.

Chapter 1
Researching Suppliers

Finding the right supplier is where we separate the boys from the men, the wantrepreneur to the entrepreneur, and the wannabe boss to the serious business owner. Why? Because it's the part where you put your money where your mouth is. Now it's time to actually invest a few hundred dollars to a few thousand dollars for your first inventory. So, we want to make this right and make sure that we don't make the all too common mistakes most newbie ecommerce sellers make.

The Dangers of Choosing the Wrong Supplier

1 – You'll lose time & money

If you get the wrong supplier, then you'll have a really miserable time because you'll probably lose money. You can pick an unreliable supplier and extend the process for months and months with nothing to show for it. You may pick a supplier who's just outsourcing the manufacturing to other bigger suppliers. You may get lots of additional hidden costs that you're not expecting. Heck, you may even get scammed by a supplier. All of these things may happen and you need to be 100% sure that you are dealing with a legit supplier.

2 – You'll quit

More painful than losing time & money is the act of quitting the business.

After all the work you've put in so far, the capital you invested and the effort you put working on the business may be for nothing if you quit because you lost your shirt and you lost trust in the process because of dealing with the wrong supplier.

Trust me, I know dozens of new sellers who quitted because of how painful the experience has been dealing with the wrong supplier.

So, what do you need to check to be sure that you are only working with a legit supplier?

What to Look for in a Supplier

1 – Legit Operations

First, check if the company has a website (and they should have one!). If you're using Alibaba, HKTDC or the other platforms that I'm going to show you later, they should have a company profile that shows different aspects of their business.

Stuff like the type of business they have, their company address, trademarks, product certifications, number of employees and the year they were established.

Business Type	Manufacturer, Other	Country / Region	Guangdong, China
Main Products	Wireless Microphone, Speaker, Wired Microphone	Total Employees	11 - 50 People
Total Annual Revenue	Below US$1 Million	Year Established	2016
Certifications		Product Certifications(6)	CE, CE, ROHS, CE, CE, ROHS
Patents(1)	wireless microphone(B7)	Trademarks(1)	BAOBAOMI
Main Markets	Southeast Asia 26.00% North America 10.00% Domestic Market 10.00%		

[Image 1.1]

It's not that hard to find these details and it's definitely worth the time researching them and confirming if these are true.

What I like about using Alibaba, HKTDC, TTNET and other platforms is their verification process. They have a reputation to uphold and they won't just allow any supplier to sell on their platform.

2 – Client Feedback and Online Reputation

Another thing to look at are their client's feedback and their online reputation in general. For client feedback, read the reviews they are getting on their profile or product pages. The more positive feedback they have, the better.

Also, Google their company and make sure that they do not have any pending cases or complaints. Not all companies will have 100% happy customers but you should try to find a company that has zero bad records if possible.

3 – Years in Business

You can also find the number of years they have been operating as a manufacturer. This is important because you want someone who already knows the entire process of how all of this works. You don't want to be their guinea pig as they try to navigate starting their own manufacturing business. As a rule of thumb, I only work with manufacturers who already has at least 4-5 years of experience in the business.

4 – Customization Availability

Make sure that they allow product customization as well. If you are doing a private label product, it is crucial that you have some kind of differentiation from your competition. Most manufacturers will allow branding but that's just the first step.

Can they offer different colors? Can they create a different mold? Are they open to changing some aspects of the product so it can match your vision?

Work with someone who's open to all of these things because you cannot dominate FBA if you're just selling a "me too" products without any differentiation at all.

5 – Product Availability

This is an obvious one. Always confirm to them if they can make that specific product and if they have the available resources to do so. Some companies will say yes but will then outsource to other manufacturers. Never ever deal with a manufacturer who has to pass the product creation part to other companies. You have to make sure that you're dealing with them directly so you'll have full control of what the final product may look like.

6 – The Numbers Make Sense

We are doing this because we want to make money. So, the numbers have to make sense. If you are getting the product at $3 each, you must be able to sell it for at least $15 on Amazon. Anything less would probably result in a net loss.

To avoid losing money, I always follow the 5X Rule.

The 5X rule states that you must be able to sell the product at 5x its manufacturing cost so you can at least break even.

There are other expenses that you have to think about like shipping, FBA fees, selling fees, and product inspection (which we'll talk about in chapter 4). All of those things may add up and following the 5X rule puts you on a safe side and allows you to at the very least, breakeven. Obviously, it's all different and it will still depend on the product that you are selling. But as a general rule, I just go to Amazon first and compared what price is the product selling at and how much does it cost per quantity to produce.

For example, if this BBQ gloves sell for $3.25 in Alibaba, then I must be able to sell it on Amazon for at least $16.25. (please see images 1.2 and 1.3 for reference)

(Image 1.2)

(Image 1.3)

The key here is to find a product on Amazon that is as close to the one you are looking at on Alibaba or other manufacturing platforms.

7 – Willingness to Negotiate

You'll never really know this until later in the process. For now, just keep in mind that pro-sellers will always be willing to negotiate a win-win deal so you guys can make a long-term business relationship.

8 – Badges

Most manufacturing platforms will have some kind of badge that shows social proof and the legitimacy of the manufacturing company.

Later, I'll explain them in detail and I'll show you the most important ones to look at.

9 – Response Time & Quality of Response

Another important thing is their response time. Are they getting back to you within 12-48 hours or do they usually take 4-5 days to reply?

I only deal with suppliers who always get back to me within 48 hours.

Now, it's not just enough that they get back to me on time. It's also important that their response actually answers my questions and concerns.

10 – Lead Time & Shipping Time

Lead time is the number of days or weeks it takes for them to finish manufacturing your product. Setting the right expectation and communication is the key here. If they say that they need at least 4 weeks to manufacture your Christmas related product and its already November 20, then you probably won't make the cut since you still have to do the shipping which usually takes 7-45 days depending on the option you choose. By the time your Christmas related product appears on your Amazon store, it would already be too late since it'll most likely already be January.

Remember this simple formula, **lead time + shipping time = product availability date on Amazon.**

11 – Payment Options

Make sure that they have lots of payment options available. I never ever do Western Union since it can get sketchy when it comes to tracking that payment.

For a safer payment, you can do VISA, Mastercard, Apple Pay, and PayPal instead.

(Image 1.4)

12 – They Already Deal with Other FBA Sellers

It boggles my mind that new FBA sellers don't ask their supplier if they already have some kind of experience with other FBA sellers. Asking this simple question will save you lots of time and headache in the process. If you're dealing with a company that already manufactures and ships for other FBA sellers, then you're in luck because they already know what to do and they can also educate you on how all of these works.

This is not a requirement per se, but dealing with a manufacturer with lots of experience with other FBA sellers will result in a more likely positive experience for you.

****

In the next part of this chapter (as well as in chapters 2 & 3), I'll show you how you can apply all of these and how you can use these 12 criteria when searching for a supplier. I'll give you some examples, screenshots, templates and an explanation on why I picked a specific supplier as well.

5 WAYS TO FIND A SUPPLIER

A - Google Search

I know this is pretty obvious, but I recommend that this is where you start. Just search on Google and find potential suppliers that matches your product.

Here are some examples + keyword terms to use:

1 – Product Name + Supplier

Just type your product name + add the word "supplier" in it.

boardmarker supplier

(Image 1.5)

You will likely see lots of websites offering the product you are looking for. Sometimes, they will be independent website or the supplier's website. Other times, you will see supplier listings from Alibaba, HKTDC and other big manufacturing platforms.

About 119,000 results (0.47 seconds)

www.made-in-china.com › ... › Marker & Highlighter ▾

White Board Marker manufacturers & suppliers - Made-in ...

China White **Board Marker manufacturers** - Select 2020 high quality White Board Marker products in best price from certified Chinese Marker manufacturers, ...

www.officewarehouse.com.ph › product ▾

Schneider White Board Marker 290 #129001 Black 1-3mm ...

Your Office Solutions **Provider** ... Schneider White **Board Marker** 290 #129002 Red 1-3mm; Schneider White **Board Marker** 290 #129003 Blue 1-3mm; Schneider ...

www.alibaba.com › ... › marker › board marker

Board Marker Set Wholesale, Board Marker Suppliers - Alibaba

Good quality bulk stationery **supply** 12pcs marker white **board marker** pen set >> Product detail Our service 1) Conforms CE,EN71-1,-2,-3,-9 and ASTM ...

www.alibaba.com › ... › China board marker ink ▾

China board marker ink - Alibaba.com

China **Board Marker** Ink, China **Board Marker** Ink **Suppliers** and **Manufacturers** Directory - Source

(Image 1.6)

2 – Product Name + Private Label

If you are looking to sell a private label product with your own brand, you can also use the search term "private label" after your product name.

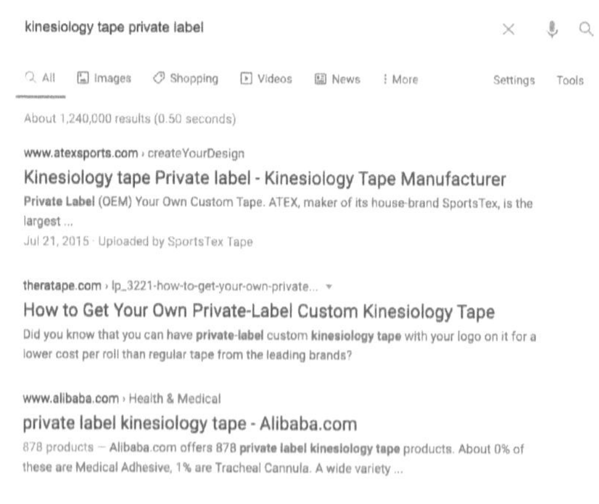

(Image 1.7)

3 – Product Name + Country/State + (manufacturer or private label)

If you want to source locally (assuming you're in the U.S.), then you just have to add the state you want to choose. I recommend that you search for your own state or the state near you first so shipping samples would be easier.

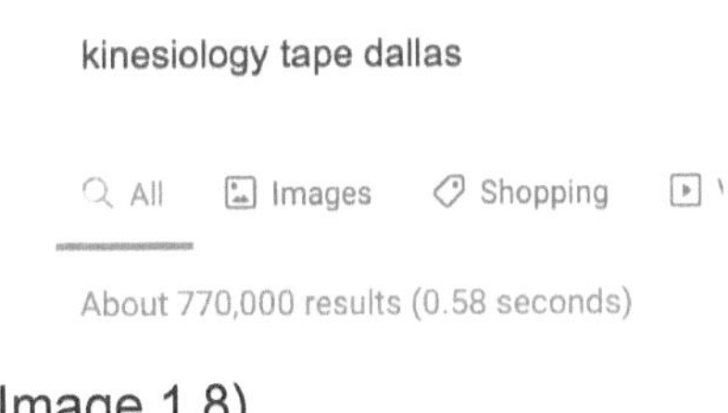

(Image 1.8)

You can also add the word "manufacturer" or "private label" after the state to make your search more specific.

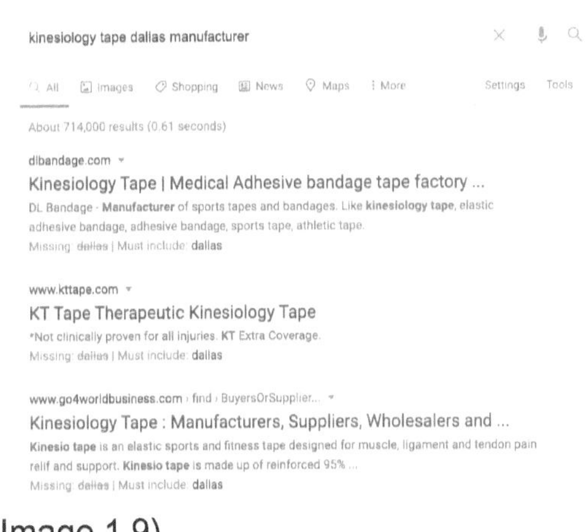

(Image 1.9)

Another thing that you need to consider is the type of product you are selling.

Let's say that you want to sell something that is made from coconut. Try to think about the countries where coconut grows and where this product may be created cheaper.

In this case, the Philippines would be a good choice since they literally have unlimited coconuts there and it is a big source of income and livelihood for the people there.

In this case, your keyword may be your product name + manufacturer + Philippines.

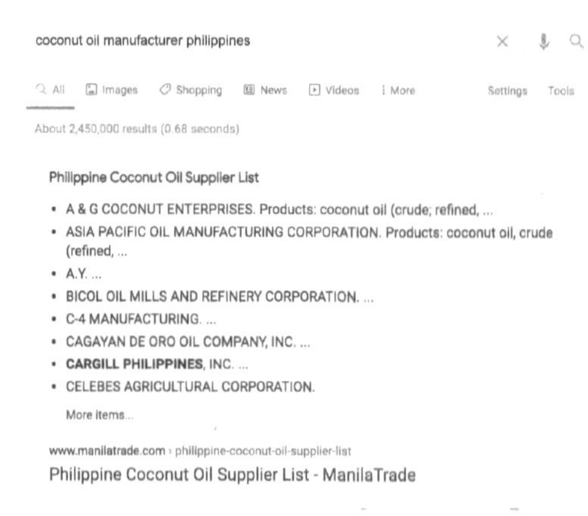

(Image 1.10)

Try to think outside the box and don't limit yourself to just manufacturing in China. There are literally dozens of options out there and you just have to be strategic about your research so you can make the best decision for your business.

4 – Product Name + Manufacturer

This is self-explanatory so I'm not going to spend much time on this. It's as simple as searching for your product name + the word "manufacturer" in it.

BIG TIP: Always Go Through the Top 50 Results from Google

Suppliers aren't always good at marketing themselves, especially with SEO. I recommend that you go through the top 20-50 results because you may find suppliers that aren't really doing SEO but are still awesome with what they do nonetheless.

B – Alibaba

About 70% of the products I sell on Amazon came from Alibaba. I don't particularly think it's because Alibaba is better than other platforms. It's because I was able to build a solid win-win and long-term relationship with the suppliers that I already have.

If you're just getting started, I recommend that you also start with Alibaba. They are the largest aggregator of manufacturers coming from China. 99% of the time, you'll find what you want to sell on Amazon in Alibaba.

For Alibaba, I just start with the keyword related to my product. For example: Yoga Mat

I would also search for Alibaba's suggested keywords as they will add other potential suppliers that offer the same thing.

(Please refer to image 1.11)

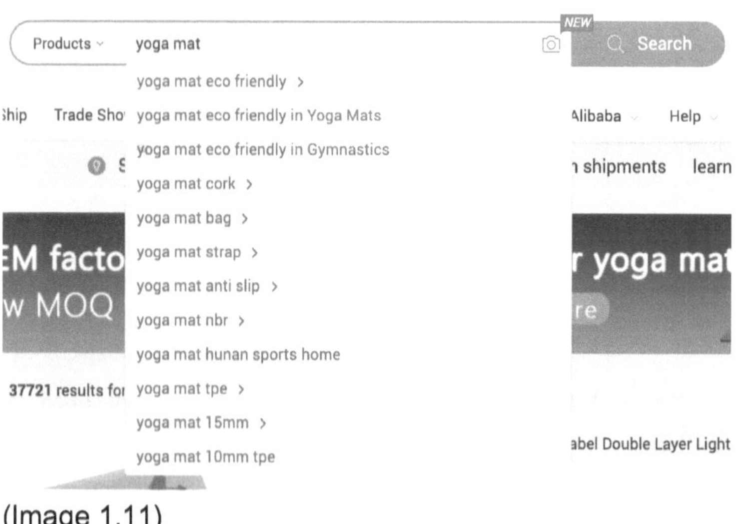

(Image 1.11)

I like to see the following when I'm searching on Alibaba:

1 – Complete Trade assurance, certifications, and verified supplier

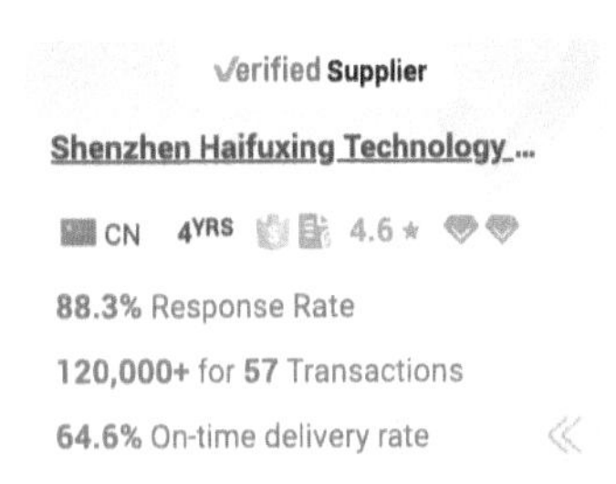

(Image 1.12)

2 – They should have more than 4 years experience manufacturing that product.

(Image 1.13)

This means they have lots of experience and they are more likely to be easier to work with.

3 - They should have more than 70% response rate

(Image 1.14)

This means they are serious and they are answering people's questions fast.

4 – Complete details

I would like to see a lot of information about their company and about their product. You must take some time to read and understand all of it. I know, it's hard and it takes some time, but it's worth it. All of these are important.

Read their company profile. Look at their website, company history, online reputation, supplier reputation index (this should be at least 2 diamonds) and other relevant information that makes their operation legit.

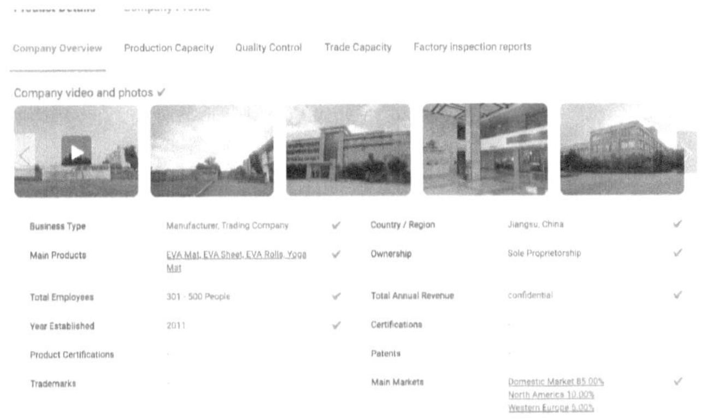

(Image 1.15)

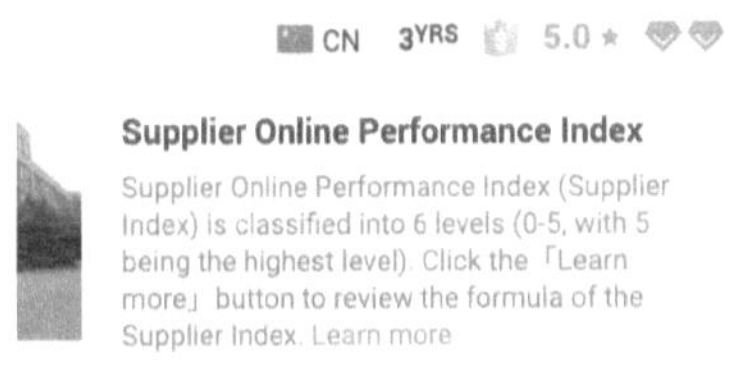

(Image 1.16)

5 - 5x rule

If the manufacturing cost per unit is not at least 4x or 5x the price you can sell it for, then ditch it. For example, if the price per unit of a yoga mat is $5 on Alibaba, then make sure that you can sell it for $25 and above on Amazon.

6 – Delivery Rate

Another crucial information to look at is their delivery rate.

I only work with companies that has at least 80% on-time delivery rate.

200,000+ for **180** Transactions
95.5% On-time delivery rate

(Image 1.17)

Less than that and I'll be very cautious on working with that manufacturer.

CN   **3YRS**   5.0 ★
44.4% On-time delivery rate

(Image 1.18)

C – TTNET.NET

I love this resource because they can give you a lot of different products to choose from and different choices of the product's origin country.

Simply search for your product and you'll find a lot of suppliers ready to talk to you via email/chat/or phone.

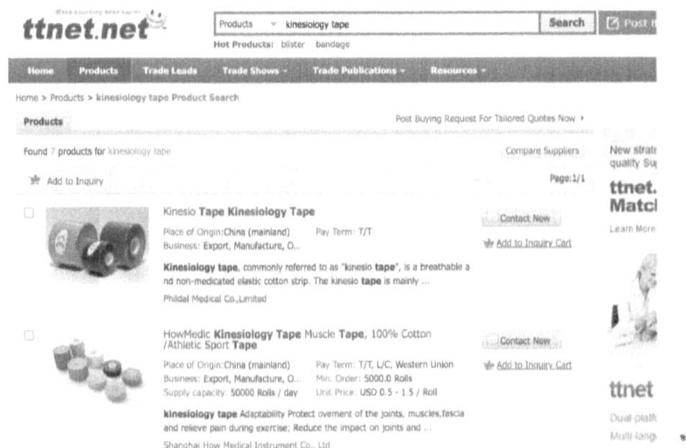

(Image 1.19)

When you are looking for a supplier, make sure that you only deal with the MANUFACTURER and not a trading company.

You can usually find this detail in the product listing but it wouldn't hurt to ask them directly about it. Make it clear that you only want to work with a direct supplier and NOT a trading company.

Product Category:	Adhesive Tapes/n.e.s.
Sales Method:	Export, Manufacture, OEM/ODM
Payment Term:	T/T

(Image 1.20)

AGAIN, ONLY DEAL WITH THE MANUFACTURER.

Wholesalers & Trading companies will add 15-20% to your total Cost of goods sold. Not cool.

In addition, read everything that you can about this company, especially if you plan to do a lot of business with them.

It would also be smart to Google search them and find their websites. Most of these guys in TTNET don't show their website. So you have to do more research.

Also, it would be nice to know their specialty. You only want the best and your customers deserves only the best.

D - HKTDC

Another awesome place to find products is HKTDC.

(Image 1.21)

They have a lot of suppliers from Hongkong, China, and Taiwan.

It's pretty much the same as TTNET, you just have to search for your product and look at different suppliers that may have your product available for production.

When you do your research, make sure that you click on the **Product & Services** option.

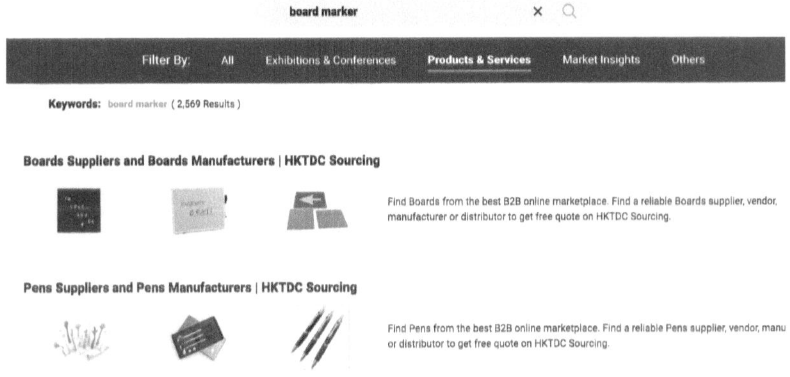

(Image 1.22)

Click on one of the results and then use this criteria for your search.

Tick on "Verified Supplier" for the supplier type.

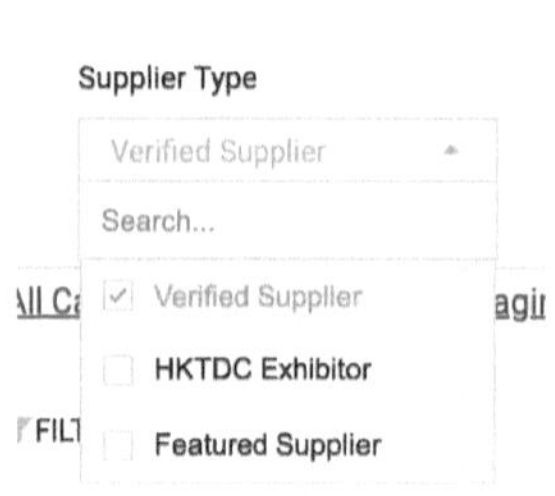

(Image 1.23)

Then choose the country or region that you want to use. I suggest that you just click on all of them, and do the same for factory location.

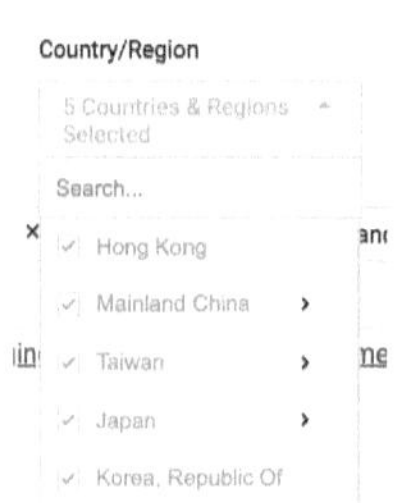

(Image 1.24)

(Image 1.25)

For nature of business, I only tick on "manufacturer" so I get to do business directly with the supplier.

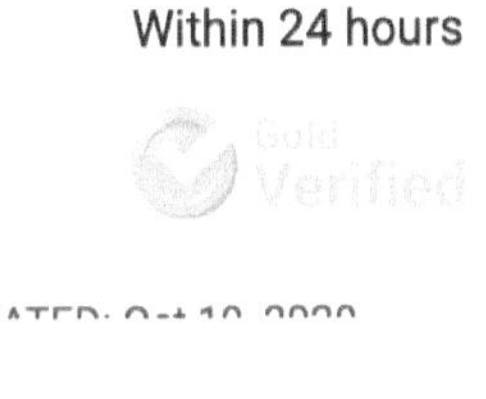

(Image 1.26)

Choosing any other "nature of business" may lead to higher cost and you want to avoid that especially if you're just getting started.

You may also want to consider only working with manufacturers with GOLD or SILVER verification. This shows that they are a real company with a good reputation.

(Image 1.27)

Don't forget to check more details about their business just like what you did with Alibaba and TTNET.

E - Ask Your Social Media Friends

The last option that I recommend is to try and ask your social media friends about potential supplier for the product that you want to sell. Sometimes, a simple post on Facebook or your Instagram story can lead to the best supplier for your product.

It wouldn't really hurt to try and ask publicly. If no one recommends anyone, then just delete your post – no harm done – and move on to using other ways of searching for a supplier.

Chapter 2
Hiring the Best Suppliers

One of the best ways to increase profit margin is to work with the right supplier. You can't just pick anybody that has the best prices. It's a good start but that shouldn't define who you ultimately work with.

For example, I once worked with a supplier from China for a plastic made gym bottle that I used to sell years ago. At first glance, that supplier looks shiny and awesome – they have the best numbers and I'm going to make $3 more profits per item if I went with them. Mind you, I sell around 500 pieces per month at that time so that's an extra $1,500 per month (in addition to the original profit I already calculated) in my pocket that I can use to my bling bling and stuff. The problem was they are a little bit of a pain in the butt to work with. Most of them have a hard time following instruction, some of the people I talked to can hardly understand english, and they tend to reply very late. This could've been an awesome deal but there's so many red flags that I have to weigh-in. At the same time, I also found another Chinese manufacturer that offers it at a higher price and it would only make me an extra $1.5 per piece or an extra $750 per month. However, this seller replies fast, has a better track record, delivers on time and they always message me about stuff related to the product.

Guess who I chose to work with? The second one.

Yes, I made less money but I was also able to have less stress and save more time because of how good they are as a seller and manufacturer. Remember, it's not solely about the profits. It's also about having a good long-term business relationship.

I ended up working with the second manufacturer for the last 4 years and I was also able to save lots of time and money because I already have a reliable company to work with on a long-term basis.

THE PURPOSE OF PRE-RESEARCH

The goal of this chapter is to show you how to do preliminary research so you won't waste your time talking to them for hours and hours only to find out that they are not capable of being your supplier.

We want to make this process seamless and repeatable because you're going to do this over and over again until you find your perfect supplier match.

Here are the 4 preliminary steps you have to do before you hire a supplier and make your first big order.

Step 1 – Find and Save

The first step is to just find suppliers and save their information on a spreadsheet.

I recommend that you create a supplier spreadsheet so you'll be able to track everything that you're doing. By having some kind of spreadsheet, you'll know exactly who you already contacted, what things you said, and other important stuff you need to take note of.

Having a spreadsheet also allows you to see the information in an organized way, which then allows you to make a better decision on who to ultimately work with.

SUPPLIER NAME	CATEGORY	timezone	contact name	email	phone #	skype

I	J	K	L	M	N
moq	leadtime	volume available	date contacted		NOTES?\

(Image 2.1)

For starters, I recommend inputting the following information:

A – Supplier/Manufacturer Company Name

B – Product Name or Product Category

C – Contact Name

D – Contact Email/Skype/Contact Number

E – Minimum Order Quantity They Are Asking For (Note: This is almost always negotiable)

D – Lead Time (This is the number of days or weeks they need to produce the product not including the shipping time)

E – Volume Available (This is the quantity of unit they can produce per month)

F – Date Contact

G – Additional Notes

Do this so you'll never lose track of what's happening with the relationship between you and the supplier.

Step 2 – Making the First Contact, Qualifying, and Getting Price Quotes

I swear, a lot of new sellers treat the first contact as if they're finding hookups on Tinder. They're too casual and they don't command any respect at all.

"Hey, how you doin'?"

"Hi, can you customize this product? How much do I have to pay per piece?"

"Hey, can you sell this product for 200 MOQ instead and lower the price by $1 each?"

The problem with this half-hearted approach is they do not appear professional and they are full of incomplete details necessary to make a buying decision.

From the very first contact, you should have an air of professionalism and they should feel like they are working with a pro.
You want them to feel that they are working with a million-dollar company even if you're only operating in your garage.

Here's an example of the first message I send to manufacturers:

Hi,

My name is Red, a manager and purchasing agent of Ecom X Company LLC.

I am reaching out to inquire about the possibility of working together and creating a long-term business relationship. We are an international e-commerce company based on Los Angeles, California and we are interested in some of the products you offer.

We're looking for a nationwide manufacturer of a product similar to this link:

Amazon.com/productlink
Product dimensions: 2 x 4
Weight: 1lb
Shipping Weight: 1.25lb

Kindly answer the following questions about your product:

#1 – What is the cost of the product per unit including custom packaging (+ our logo) with an order of 500 units, 1,000 units and 2,000 units?

#2 – Can you print our logo in your product?

#3 – Can you provide custom packaging solutions?

#4 – Can you put the UPC in the product?

#5 – Are you able to send a custom sample of the product and how much would you charge if sent via DHL or FedEx to the following address: Your address here

Thank you and I'm looking forward to hearing from you soon,

Red, Lead Product Manager at Ecom X Company

**

This simple message alone can help you separate yourself from other sellers who just message short but unserious-like messages to the manufacturers.

Note: Please don't copy this word for word. However, I do want you to follow the structure of the message.

The key here is to act professional and find out the preliminary details necessary for you to make a better buying decision later.

Another thing to remember: This is not the time to negotiate. That happens a little later in the process when you're ready to make your first big unit order. For now, focus on making sure that the supplier you chose can indeed deliver the product to you the way you want it to.

Step 4 – Requesting Product Samples

Once you already received a reply and you already calculated the numbers (just use the 5X rule) – the next step is to order samples so you can make sure that you have a quality product.

When you order a sample, make sure that it's already what the final product may look like (maybe except for the packaging as this may take time, more money and some back & forth to do). At this point, you just want to know what the actual product would look and feel like when you use it. The packaging itself can later be inspected via HD pictures and videos that your supplier may send you.

Before you order samples, you have to be clear on what you want.

Do you want to add your logo in your product? Where do you want to add it? Are there some type of iterations or differentiations that you want to add to your own private label? You have to know what those things are even before you order a sample.

The sample product will naturally cost you more because you're making them create something with some customization in it. On average, you should expect to pay between $50-$100 for the sample and it should take around 2-4 weeks to get delivered. If you're adding lots of other customization, then it'll be more expensive and you should expect the cost per unit to go up.

Note: I DO NOT recommend that you don't order any sample. Your sample is a crucial part of the process and knowing what kind of product you have can help you decide later on whether to order a large quantity or not.

Chapter 3

Ordering Units, Negotiating for the Best Prices, and the Shipping Process Explained

At this point, you already know the supplier you want to work with. You already have an idea of what your final product would look like, and you are 100% sure that this is the path that you want to take. There shouldn't be any doubt in your mind that this is indeed the product that you want to sell. If so, then you have to go back to product research.

Now it's time to make the order, and more importantly, make the correct order.

Step 1 – Know Thy Units

This is super easy but important nonetheless. First, you have to have an idea of how much you are willing to invest. If Minimum Order Quantity (MOQ) is 500 pieces and it cost $5 per piece, then you better be sure that you have $2,500 to invest – and that's just for the product itself. Remember, you also have to pay for shipping, which is usually around 10%-25% of the total cost of the product itself.

Step 2 – Negotiate MOQ & Price

Here's the mindset that I want you to have when it comes to negotiating the MOQ and/or the price per piece.

NEGOTIATE FOR LONG TERM MUTUALLY BENEFICIAL RELATIONSHIP.

It must be win-win or else, they will harbor ill will even if they ended up working with you.

The first message that you sent (remember that intro message from chapter 2?) will have a big impact on your negotiation. If you appear serious and professional from the onset, then they will respect you. If you appear and sound like a noob, then they will probably pass up on your business.

Now, the price quote that you got from them will usually be the highest price. In fact, they expect you to negotiate.

So how do we actually negotiate a win-win solution?

First, remember that you and the manufacturer have to make a profit for that transaction.

I recommend that you send a counter offer with a price and MOQ that you want to target + your profit computation.

For example, if you want to order 500 pieces of BBQ gloves at $3 each, let them know about your target profit per piece.

Usually, I would put all my expenses for the product including shipping, FBA fees, marketing fees, and every other fee I can think of. Although that wouldn't necessarily be super accurate, I want to let them know that I am only making "this much" profit per piece – and that's the reason why you're negotiating for a better price.

If you show them that after all the expenses, you're only making $2 profit per piece – then they will be more in tuned to negotiate because they know that you're not really making any money from the deal.

At first, you do this strategy and you negotiate based on logic.

Once you already have a good relationship with them, then you can blatantly ask for discounts just because you want to increase your profit margin. Even then, you can always use the same strategy and use numbers for negotiating a better deal.

Now sometimes, the price that they will give you is the best that they can do. Don't try to bargain too hard especially in the beginning. Your goal at this point is to try to move the needle a little.

Again, you have to think WIN-WIN.

If the left-hand wins, then the right hand must win as well.

Step 3 – The Shipping Process Explained

Now I'm going to explain the incredibly misunderstood world of product shipping. A little bit of a warning though, you will not learn everything that there is to know about shipping in this book. The truth is, there will be some things that you just have to learn by actually doing the real thing. However, I'm going to try my best to explain this in a relatively simple, step by step manner.

THE PROCESS:

Once your manufacturer has finished creating the product, did the inspection and it's ready to ship – they will now send the product to their port (for example, from China factory to one of their city's port). From there, it will either be loaded via airplane (air) or a container ship (sea).

From there, it will reach either an airport or a domestic seaport in the U.S.
Once it arrives, U.S. Customs (or whatever country you are in) will inspect the product. Expect this to add a 1-2 weeks delay in the shipping process. The time itself totally depends on a lot of factors like the type of product you are selling and even the season we are currently in. Electronic product usually takes more time to inspect and the Christmas season are usually the busiest months and you should expect your product to have delays during these months (usually November to January).

At this point, all you can do is check your tracking number for updates and the progress of your shipping.

Once the inspection is complete, you can either use a freight forwarder for them to handle the shipping for you or you can send it to your home address or the AMAZON FBA Warehouse itself.

So that is pretty much the entire sequence of shipping from the manufacturer to your doorstep.

Now, allow me to discuss the shipping options and all the minutia of the whole process. Knowing the meaning of shipping terms will absolutely help you clarify the right option for your situation.

Remember, you can mention these to your supplier and if they are a pro, then will understand what these means.

TYPES OF SHIPPING TO USE PART 1: Ex Works, Freight on Board, and Delivery Duty Paid

A - Ex Works or EXW

EXW is when you bear the responsibility of shipping from your supplier's warehouse to their shipping port, to your country's port, and then to your desired address/or the Amazon warehouse. You'll basically do all the work and talk to all the parties that needs to attend to your shipment. Simply put: This is the shipping method for anyone who wants to make their life a living hell.

I absolutely DO NOT recommend using this shipping method unless you hate yourself.

B - Freight on Board or FOB

This is where you share the responsibility of shipping the product with your supplier 50/50. With FOB, your supplier will handle the shipping from their warehouse all the way to your domestic port. From there onwards, you will be 100% responsible for getting it from the port to your address or Amazon's warehouse. Alternatively, you can also hire a freight forwarder to do this for you.

I recommend this method for a little more experienced sellers since it's like the happy middle for saving money and making the items arrived on time.

C - Delivery Duty Paid – DDP

DDP is when the seller is responsible for shipping the product from their warehouse to your doorstep or to Amazon's warehouse. Naturally, this will be more expensive and this may eat out your profits. However, I still recommend that you go for this if the numbers still make sense.

What you have to remember is cheaper isn't always better. Sure, you can save money from doing EXW or FOB – but the fastest way to make money from FBA is to make sure that your products are available for sale in the first place. You cannot make money with a product that isn't there. I know…DUHH… But when you're making these types of decisions, I don't want you to think only about the upfront cost. Think about the opportunity cost as well. The time you spent dealing with shipping could be spent actually marketing the product and having it already LIVE and available for sale on Amazon.

In the beginning, I can understand the hesitation to put more money into the shipping process. Trust me, I do understand the pain of spending more money and having less profit margin for my first product. But you have to think long-term and you have to use this as an opportunity to learn instead.

And that kids, is my long-winded way of saying: Just stick to Delivery Duty Paid (DDP) - or at the very least, FOB.

TYPE OF SHIPPING TO USE PART 2: AIR VS. SEA VS. LAND

The next thing you need to think about is whether you will ship your product by air, by sea, or in some cases, by land.

Truth be told, the best way will almost always be the fastest – which is by air. Almost all types of product can be ship by air unless your product is as big as a car – then in that case, the best option is by sea.

Here are some of the pros of cons of shipping by air, sea, or land.

A - SHIPPING BY AIR

- In most cases, shipping by air is the fastest. Unless there's a customs delay (which rarely happens), then you should expect your product to arrive in between 5-7 days.
- If you use a company like DHL, FedEx, or the UPS then you won't need to use a freight forwarder since these are end-to-end solutions for shipping. If you use UPS, it will typically be at around 7-12 days. Faster shipping allows you to start selling sooner but it may also eat up your profits.
- The one drawback to shipping by air is it is usually the more expensive option.

B - SHIPPING BY SEA

- Shipping by sea is the cheapest option.
- It's awesome for larger shipments.
- But it may take 21-45 days to get delivered, and that's assuming no delay from customs.
- Also, shipping by sea requires you to have a freight forwarder.

C – SHIPPING BY LAND

- This is only available if you're getting your product within the country. Just ask your manufacturer to deliver it to your desired shipping address, and voila – you're in business.
- The shipment may take between 3-14 days to arrive.

How to Save Money

If this is a new product you're selling to the market, then I suggest that you split your shipment by AIR and SEA 50/50.

Shipping by air allows you to start selling sooner which helps you establish a brand and start getting higher rankings on Amazon's search engine. Then shipping the other half by sea allows you to save money thus increasing your profit margins.

If you do this, try to make the order at the same time so the other half of the inventory may arrive by day 30 to day 60.

When Do You Need a Freight Forwarder?

If you chose FOB, then you are going to need a freight forwarder. A forwarder is basically an agent or company that handles the shipping for you once the items arrived at your local air or sea port. They will make the inspections for you and they will basically do all the paperwork and they will send the product to your preferred destination (most of the time, it's on Amazon's warehouse).

Here are some Freight Forwarders to consider:

The Establishment: **FedEx, UPS, DHL**

Forest Shipping – They specialize in FBA, so they are highly recommended. https://forestshipping.com/
OOCL - https://www.oocl.com/eng/Pages/default.aspx
MATSON - http://www.matson.com.cn/

Also, don't be afraid to ask recommendations and questions to your supplier. Most of the time, they are already working with forwarders and then can even give you a discount because you already have a connection.

HOW TO SHIP DIRECTLY TO AN AMAZON FBA WAREHOUSE

This is the path that I recommend you take whether you chose FOB or Delivery Duty Paid.

If you're 100% sure about the quality of your product; you've seen the inspection and you trust your seller with all your hard-earned investment, then it's a good idea to just ship it directly to Amazon's FBA warehouse. It'll add a bit more step in the process but it's well worth the effort and time you'll put into it.

Here's how it works step by step:

Step 1 – Know Your Shipping Option

Step 1 is to know your shipping option. **You can either ship the product to your home or business address or you can ship it directly to Amazon's warehouse.** I highly recommend that you go for the second option. This will make things easier for you. It will also allow you be hands-off when it comes to the shipping process. Now, make sure that the product was inspected properly before you choose this method.

2 – Understand What Labels You Need

To send the shipment directly to Amazon's warehouse, you will need the following:

A – UPC Code. This needs to be in all of your products and it is highly recommended that you use a box design.

B – Carton Label. This is the label that appear at the top of your Master Carton. This is the label that Amazon scans when it arrives in their warehouse.

C – FSNKU. This is an Amazon Specific Label and you need a UPC to get it.

3 – Follow the Amazon Shipping Plan

Step 1 – Go to your Sellers Central account.

Step 2 – Go to Manage Inventory

Step 3 – Choose the product box that you set up for your listing and then click on SEND/REPLENISH INVENTORY.

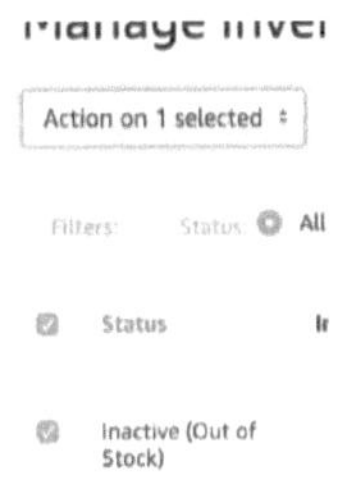

(Image 3.1)

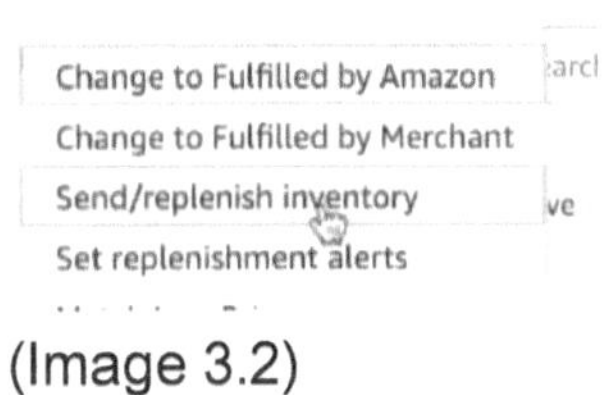

(Image 3.2)

Step 4 – Setup the Ship from Address

Ask your supplier for their full address and input it in the ship from section.

(Image 3.2)

Step 5 – Choose Your Packaging Type

And then choose "case-packed products"

Case-packed products are items that has identical items that has matching SKUs, and each case must have the same number of products. Your supplier should already know how this works so make sure that you ask them about it.

Now, multiple cases can be packed into a larger box called Master Carton, which does not qualify as case-packed and must be split into cases.

Another thing to remember is the word "unit per case" – This refers to the number of items per case and NOT the number of cases per Master Carton.

Okay, this may all sound weird and complicated, but trust me – this will all make sense once you start to actually ship your items and once you start working with your supplier.

Step 6 – Set Quantity

The next step is to set the quantity of your product. Kindly refer to image 3.4 for an example.

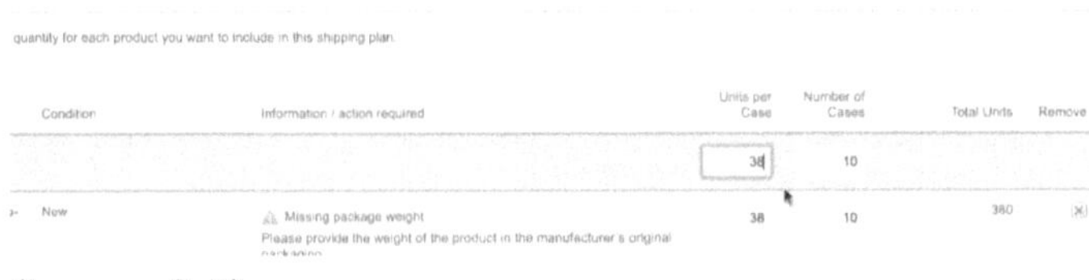

(Image 3.4)

Step 7 – Go to "Prepare Products" section and then click on the show ASIN/FNSKU checkbox. Next, choose "Merchant".

(Image 3.5)

Step 8 – Click on Print labels for this page.

(Image 3.6)

A pdf file will appear and this is the file that you should send to your supplier, to be included in the shipment itself. They will know what to do with this file as long as you clarify that this product goes directly to Amazon.

Step 9 – Review your shipment and choose SMALL
PACKAGE DELIVERY or SPD.

(Image 3.7)

Step 10 – Confirm the details that you input about your
product (weight, numbers of units, etc.)

(Image 3.8)

Step 11 – Print your box labels and then complete the
shipment.

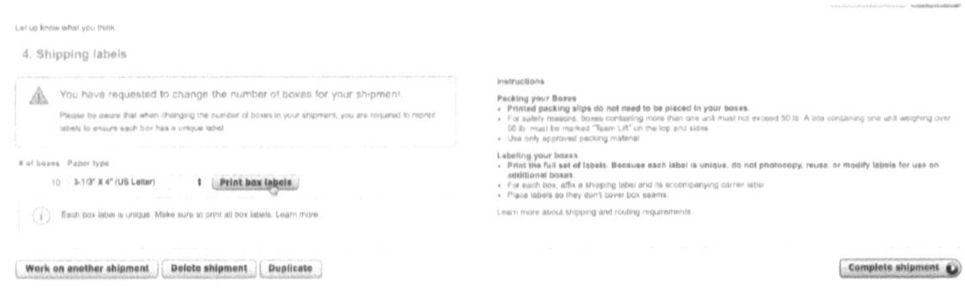

(Image 3.9)

Make sure that you save the box labels that will appear and send that as well to your supplier.

You will get something similar to this: (please refer to image 3.10)

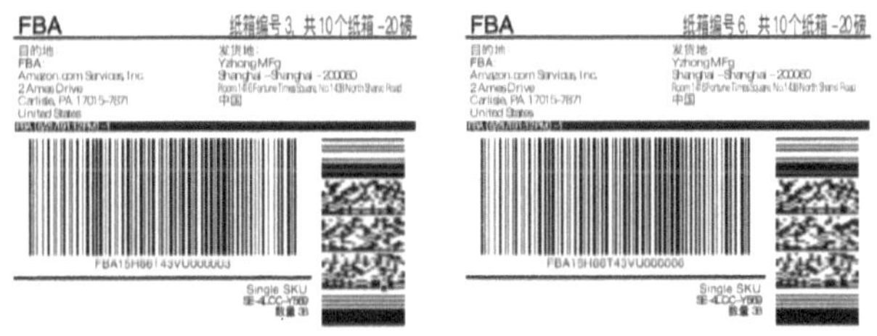

(Image 3.10)

And that's it, you now have completed the process of shipping directly to Amazon's warehouse. Just send all the printed labels to your supplier and they will already know what to do with it.

P.S. If you want a more detailed breakdown on how shipping works, I highly recommend this pdf that was provided by Amazon.

https://images-na.ssl-images-amazon.com/images/G/01/fba-help/QRG/FBA-Shipping-Inventory-to-Amazon.pdf

You can also Google "Amazon FBA shipping guide pdf" if this link didn't work.

Supplier Cheat Sheet – What You Need to Know Before Your First Order

This is the exact cheat sheet that I use for my own business.

You should have the details for all of them before you go through the initial order.

You will get most of the details in the process of talking, researching and negotiating with your supplier.

1 – Name of Supplier

2 – All contact details (email, phone #, skype etc.)

3 – Website

4 – Complete address

5 – Minimum order quantity (MOQ)

6 – What are their packaging and labeling options

7 – Do they do product customization?

8 – Lead time

9 – Shipping Options/methods

10 – Price quotes for MOQ

11- Price quotes for packaging/labeling/customization

12 – The volume of product they can create every month

13 – How does shipping works and what are the fees (from Manufacturer's factory to your warehouse /Amazon FBA - DOOR TO DOOR)

14 – Are there any additional FEES for everything? (shipping, tax, customs)

15 – How does the quality control process works

16 – The exact weight, height and every single specifications of that product

17 – What payment methods will they accept? Warning: Never ever pay via money transfer (Western Union). If they insist, run.

18 – Any possible third party options for shipping, packaging, labeling and product customization?

ADD THE FOLLOWING IF YOU'RE SHIPPING DIRECTLY TO AMAZON FBA'S WAREHOUSE:

19 – Make sure that you print (in pdf) all the labels and send it to your supplier

20 – Always inform your supplier that you are shipping directly to Amazon's warehouse.

I know that all of these may sound a lot.

But if you come to think of it, 30% of the list can be answered through your own research. The other 70% can be answered in just two 15 minute phone calls!

Also, if you really wanted to stand out in this business, talk to them via phone/skype and they will take you more seriously. When it comes to talking with suppliers, email is overrated! (Unless it's the first contact).

You'll probably be uncomfortable talking to them in the beginning, but that's alright. Would you rather be comfortable and broke? Or would you rather be uncomfortable at the beginning and eventually rich?

You decide.

P.S. While you're waiting for your product to arrive, don't mess around and just do nothing. Set up your listing sales pages, go research your keywords, and go market your potential products to future buyers.

Chapter 4

Barcodes and FBA Fees Demystified

In this chapter, I'm going to explain what barcodes are and how each type differs. I know that there's a lot of confusion when it comes to terms like UPC, FNSKU, GS1 and all of these seemingly random letters and numbers and how it relates to your Amazon business.

Let's start with the most common one:

UPC: Universal Product Code – A 12-digit barcode unique to each product.

Everything that you buy online and offline will have its own UPC unique to each product. (This is especially true in 1st world countries).

Remember the thing that the grocery store scanned when you bought your 2nd jar of peanut butter this week? That's a UPC. It's basically a tracker and a source of information for the product. Every product should have that – at least, every legal one. Different products will always have a different UPC – unless it's an illegal operation, then no two products will have the same UPC.

GS1 – Global Standards – Is the BEST and most legitimate place to buy UPC barcodes.

I used to recommend other ways to get UPC but I know better now and this is the only way that you should get one today.
Don't forget that Amazon will verify the legitimacy of your UPC by checking GS1's database. If your UPC didn't match GS1's database, then Amazon will consider it as invalid.

There are 2 ways to buy GS1's UPC.

The first one is to get it directly from GS1 via their website:

https://www.gs1.org/standards/get-barcodes

It cost $250 per 10 UPC and + $50 annual fee to register to your name or your company name.

You can also use a third party like Nationwide Barcode at a much cheaper rate at only $12 each.

https://www.nationwidebarcode.com/purchase-barcodes/barcodes-for-amazon/

It will also be cheaper if you get it by bulk. Here's the current pricing table as shown in their website.

GS1 Originated UPCs/EANs – Volume Pricing

UPC/EAN Quantity	Your Price	Total
1	$12.00	$12.00
5	$7.50	$37.50
10	$4.25	$42.50
25	$2.25	$56.25
50	$1.28	$64.00
100	$0.80	$80.00
250	$0.60	$150.00
500	$0.40	$200.00
1,000	$0.30	$300.00
2,500	$0.20	$500.00
5,000	$0.16	$800.00
10,000	$0.14	$1400.00

(Image 4.1)

They also run promos every now and then which allows you to save between 10%-40% on UPC.

Note: Do not buy from resellers on eBay, Fiverr or any other websites outside GS1 and Nationwide Barcode.

FNSKU: Fulfillment Network Stock Keeping Unit – This is Amazon's own barcode.

FNSKUs are used to track every product that goes in and out of Amazon's warehouse. These should be in every unit that you are selling.

Note: The UPC you purchased can be used to generate unique FNSKU from Amazon. Now, it is possible to use just a UPC but I highly recommend that you also generate FNSKU so Amazon will have an easier time locating and managing your product.

***

Here's how all these barcodes tied up together:

1 – You need a UPC so you can create your listing.
2 – Only purchase UPC from reliable suppliers like GS1 or Nationwide Barcode.
3 – You are allowed to only have UPC without the FNSKU but it's better to have FNSKU so Amazon can track your product better.
4 – You can generate your free FNSKU in Seller Central when you create your product listing.

I recommend reading this short blog post for more information about FNSKU.

https://www.shipcalm.com/blog/fnsku/

FBA FEES EXPLAINED:

Now let's talk about how to calculate all the FBA fees that you need to pay when you sell through Amazon FBA. You will add these to your expense column and you should also take this into account as you compute your profit per product unit sold.

The first fee to consider is the selling fee. To sell on Amazon as an individual, you can start for $0 but it's only limited to 40 items per month plus there's a $0.99 fee for every unit sold + the shipping cost. To sell on Amazon as a professional, you need to pay a monthly fee of $39.99 per month. On top of this monthly fee, these are the other ones that you have to pay if you chose to have them manage your inventory and ship the product for you.

Please refer to image 4.2 and 4.3 for reference.

#1 - Fulfillment (Shipping) Fee:

Size tier	Max dimension	Shipping weight [1]	Packaging	Fulfillment fee per unit [2]
FBA Small and Light	16" x 9" x 4"	4 oz. or less	0.7 oz.	$1.97
		4+ oz. to < 10 oz.	0.7 oz.	$2.39
Small standard	15" x 12" x 0.75"	10 oz. or less	4 oz.	$2.50
		10+ to 16 oz.	4 oz.	$2.63
Large standard	18" x 14" x 8"	10 oz. or less	4 oz.	$3.31
		10+ to 16 oz.	4 oz.	$3.48

(Image 4.2)

Depending on the weight and dimension of the product, the cost will vary from $1.97 up to an average of $5 per unit. It can go up to 100s of dollars but that's only applicable for very heavy and huge shipments.

#2 - FBA Storage Fee:

FBA storage fees *

Inventory storage fees are charged monthly based on the daily average volume (measured in cubic feet) for the space your inventory occupies in Amazon fulfillment centers. The volume measurement is based on unit size when properly packaged and ready to ship.

Month	Standard size	Oversize
January - September	$0.75 per cubic foot	$0.48 per cubic foot
October - December	$2.40 per cubic foot	$1.20 per cubic foot

(Image 4.3)

The storage fee will also depend on the dimension of your product and the month of the year as October to December are usually very busy and full-packed months for ecommerce. Expect to pay $0.75 per cubic foot of storage from January to September and $2.40 per cubic foot storage during the Holiday season.

There are some other fees that may occur depending on your product but these ones are the basic fees that you will always have to pay for if you're using FBA.

To learn more about fees, I recommend that you check out this link:

https://sell.amazon.com/pricing.html

Chapter 5
Supplier Related Practices
of the Most Profitable
Ecommerce Business Owners

By now, you already have a process of researching, evaluating, and hiring a supplier from start to finish. In this chapter, I want to give you some of the best tips that I can give when it comes to working with suppliers. All of these tips may seem generic or even common advice, but trust me, these little tips can help you a lot as you navigate the sometimes complicated (but still awesome) world of Amazon FBA.

Tip #1 – Build Long Term Win-Win Relationships

Always choose long-term over short-term wins. This may cost you a buck or two of profit in the beginning but you have to believe in win-win relationships. The manufacturer has to make their target profit per product as well. Don't worry because as you build the relationship, you'll be able to ask for more discounts and you'll be able to negotiate better prices. Most manufacturers want you to stay with them for as long as possible. They understand that getting new customers is much harder than retaining one. If they are a good supplier, they will offer you the best price that they can offer – as simple as that.

Tip #2 – Calculate the Profits Conservatively + Proper Cost Evaluation

When you're doing the pre-research for the product and the supplier, be conservative with your calculations. Following the 5X rule is a safe bet for you to hit breakeven. If the product per unit cost is $3, then you have to be able to sell it for at least $15 on Amazon to hit breakeven or to profit. Remember that you'll also have other expenses like shipping cost, FBA fees, FBA storage fees, UPC, etc.

Tip #3 – Contact as Many Suppliers as Possible

It's very unlikely that you'll find your main supplier just by messaging the first supplier listing you'll see on Alibaba. The truth is, it may take tens if not hundreds of messages before you truly find that one or two suppliers that you will eventually work with for your future products. But once you found that one supplier, it'll be so worth it because they can save you lots of time, money, and even effort in making the manufacturing and shipping as seamless as possible.

I highly recommend that you message as many suppliers as you can. I know that you're tempted to just message 3 and choose the one that replies, but you have to be patient and stick to the criteria and standard that we set for ourselves. Just be patient and follow the process I laid out in this book.

Tip #4 – Clear Instructions + Confirm Things Before the Order

Always give them clear instructions whenever you are passing some kind of details about your product or shipment. If you want them to put a label on your package, then be clear and let them know exactly where to put it. Or if you don't know where to put it, ask them questions about past customers and how they did it for their own FBA shipments.

Also, make sure that you confirm details before you finalize your order. Follow the cheat sheet I gave you in chapter 3.

Tip #5 – Choose Quality Over Price

In the beginning, you will be tempted to choose price over quality. I understand what you're going through. You're nervous about not making any profit and losing your hard-earned investment. But you have to think about the customers here. If your customers are happy, then they will leave 5-star reviews and you will be able to charge a little more for your product because of the quality as well. Choosing to earn a few dollars of profit in the beginning probably means making thousands later.

Tip #6 – Address Supplier Concerns Respectfully

If you're having issues with your suppler (and trust me you will), then ask them about it respectfully. Being rude and condescending will only lead to a sour business relationship. Always be clear on where you stand, and let them know that you appreciate the work they are putting in. Then address your concern and let them know that you want X thing to be solved by a certain target date.

Tip #7 – Pay on Time

Manufacturers adore customers who always pay on time. If you say that you're going to pay 50% before x date, then pay it at least 2-3 days before that set-date.

Tip #8 – Pick the Right Shipping Method

Air shipping, although faster, isn't always better in all cases. Sometimes, shipping by sea may fit your product better (this is especially true for heavy and/or huge items). Another thing to consider is your current financial situation. Hey, if you can't afford shipping by air then by all means, go for sea shipping for now and sacrifice a little bit of time before you can sell your product on Amazon. In the beginning, you probably have more time than money anyway so there's no point in losing sleep about this.

Tip #9 – Put Everything into a Contract

I am not a lawyer and I cannot give legal advice but make sure that you put everything into a contract so you won't get taken advantage of by the supplier. The most important ones are the quality of the product and what it should look like, the price, the manufacturing lead time, and the method of shipping to be used for the package.

Conclusion

THE TRUTH ABOUT THE AMAZON FBA BUSINESS

I wish I could tell you that finding an A+ supplier is easy. I wish I could tell you that you could just pick any supplier and then you'll never have to worry about doing anything at all. But it doesn't work that way. There's a lot of tasks to be done and many people will quit along the way. You have to persevere, go through some growing pains, and learn every step of the way.

Here's a recap of the process:

Step 1 – Learn to find where the best suppliers are.

Step 2 – Hire the Best Suppliers by making the right evaluation.

Step 3 – Make the correct order, negotiate the best prices and choose the right shipping option.

Step 4 – Identify the right barcodes you need for your business and learn to calculate your FBA fees.

Step 5 – Wrap it up with the right foundation by following the best practices I recommended in chapter 5.

***

Right now, I understand that there's also a lot of temptation to just buy another Amazon FBA coaching program from tons of gurus out there. But the truth is you probably won't learn something from them that you won't already learn just by spending a few bucks buying the best-selling books on Amazon about FBA. Start with that because it's cheaper and you'll probably save more time and money since it only takes a few hours to read a book while watching a monstrous 40 hours online course will take a huge chunk of your time. I would rather have you spend that time taking action and making things happen for your business. I wish you all the best in this journey.

Talk soon,

Red

Review Request

As you might already know, reviews are the lifeblood of every author out there. If you found some value in this one, allow me to humbly ask for a review on Amazon as it does help in spreading my message.

Thank you, and good luck on your e-commerce business.

Fulfillment by Amazon for Beginners

If you like to learn a simple and step by step way of getting started with Amazon FBA, I recommend that you check out my other books AMAZON FBA Step by Step (by Red Mikhail), FBA Product Research 101 and Amazon Keyword Research 101 as well.

These are also available as audiobooks.

Just like this one, these 3 has a very simple language and conversational tone to it. If you found this book valuable, then you will like those 3 books as well.

OTHER BOOKS

I also have other books about making money online through different ways, check them out here:

Amazon's Associate Program
One Hour Dropshipping System
Amazon Product Listing Formula

AMAZON FBA FUTURE UPDATES:

We're just scratching the surface. In the next few months, I'm going to launch a series of books about:

FBA Advance Traffic & Marketing Strategies

Amazon Wholesaling

Amazon Retail Arbitrage

Amazon Dropshipping

And many more books related to Amazon FBA.

If you want to make sure that you get a notification when these books go LIVE, just simply follow my Amazon author page here:

https://www.amazon.com/Red-Mikhail/e/B00X3KJ2TO/

(Click the follow button on that page to get instant updates from Amazon)